Message in a Bottle

I Talk You Talk Press

CONTENTS

I Talk You Talk Press

CHAPTER ONE

Henri Olivier is a very rich, retired businessman. He is 85 years old. He has a private island in the Atlantic Ocean near Gran Canaria. He doesn't have many friends. He doesn't like parties. He stays on his island. He has a housekeeper. She cooks and cleans the house. The housekeeper's husband looks after the garden. Henri likes his house. It is very beautiful. Every room has long glass doors with a balcony outside. When the weather is good, Henri sits on the balcony outside his office. The balcony outside his office is high above the sea. Henri can look down to the ocean. He cannot see any land. Henri thinks his balcony is like a ship. He reads books. He looks at the ocean. He looks at sea birds.

Henri has a son. His name is Etienne. Sometimes his son comes to visit him on the island, but Henri does not like his son. When Etienne comes to the island, he always asks for money. His father always gives him some money, but Etienne always wants more.

One day in August, Etienne comes to the island. The gardener and his wife are not there. They have gone to visit their daughter.

"I want fifty-thousand Euros," says Etienne.

"No," says Henri. "I will give you five thousand Euros. And that is the end. I will not give you any more money."

He hears his son talking on his phone. His son says, "I hope my father dies soon. I want all his money."

My son does not love me, thinks Henri. *When I die, I don't want my son to get the money. I must make a plan.*

Henri talks on the phone to his lawyer in Madrid.

"Mr Berger, when I die, I don't want my son to get my money."

"OK, Mr Olivier. Who should get your money?"

"I don't know. But I don't want Etienne to get it. I want to give it to a charity. I want to give it to an animal charity."

"OK, Mr Olivier, but I need your signature. You must come to Madrid and sign the papers."

"OK, I can do that."

"How is your health?" asks Mr Berger.

"It is not so good, but I can go to Madrid. I will visit your office next week."

Henri puts the phone down.

The door opens. Etienne walks into the room. He has a bottle of wine. He has been drinking a lot.

"Who were you talking to?" asks Etienne.

"I was talking to my lawyer."

"I heard you. When you die, you are giving your money to animals. Animals? Are you crazy? You stupid old man!"

Etienne walks over to his father. He stands very close.

"Call Mr Berger. Tell him you made a mistake."

Henri looks at his son.

"No, I will not do it."

"Do it!" shouts Etienne. "Do it now!"

Etienne throws a photograph of the family across the room. It breaks on the floor.

Henri looks at Etienne. "You are a bad son. Your mother…"

Etienne walks to the glass door. He looks at the sea outside. Then he looks at his father.

"But my mother is not here. She is dead. She has been dead since I was a child. And you were a bad father."

"Etienne, stop it! Do you want me to die?"

"Yes, I do," says Etienne.

"You will not get any of my money," shouts Henri.

"Oh yeah?" says Etienne. "You have to see Mr Berger."

"I will go next week."

Etienne runs to his father and pushes him hard. "No you won't," he shouts.

Henri falls onto the floor.

"My back! My back!" shouts Henri. "I can't move!"

Etienne laughs. He sits down at his father's desk. He looks at his father's papers. "Your business!" he says. "You made so much money! But you plan to give it to animals and not to me!" He throws everything from the desk onto on the floor.

Etienne takes his father's smartphone. He opens the glass doors and walks out onto the balcony. He throws the phone down into the sea.

"You're not going anywhere. Hurry up and die." He laughs and walks to the door.

"Etienne!" Henri shouts. "When will you come back?"

Etienne looks at him. "Maybe next week."

"But I can't move!"

"Good. You will die quickly," says Etienne. "No one will come to help you. I will call your housekeeper. I will tell her you don't want her or her husband to work for you anymore."

A few minutes later, Henri hears Etienne leave the island on his speedboat.

He looks around the room. The sun is coming in through the window and he can hear the sound of the boat go farther away.

Henri tries to stand up, but he can't. His back hurts a lot and he can't move his legs.

Night comes. The only sound is the waves. Through the window he can see the lights of the mainland.

"Someone help me!" he shouts. "Someone help me!"

CHAPTER TWO

Etienne is in a bar on the mainland with his friends.

"How is your father?" asks a friend. "I can't see the lights on his island. Is he away?"

Etienne looks over the water.

"No, he's on his island. But he is not very well. He had a fall. He fell down the stairs."

"Who is looking after him?" asks the friend.

"He has help."

"I hope he gets well soon."

"Yeah," says Etienne. He smiles. "Do you want some champagne?"

The next morning, Henri wakes up. He is lying on the floor. He is cold. He needs some water. He looks at the clock. It is 5:00am. The doors to the balcony are open.

Etienne, Etienne, why are you doing this? He must not get my money, he thinks. *He must not get my money. What can I do?*

He tries to move. His legs do not move but he can use his arms. Henri has an idea.

Very slowly, he pulls his body across the floor. Everything from his desk is on the floor. Henri finds a pen and paper.

He writes on the paper in French and English.

---Help me. I'm Henri Olivier on the island. Call Mr Berger's law office in Madrid. Telephone number 0123-454-676. And call the police. Emergency! SOS!---

He moves to the kitchen and finds an empty wine bottle. He puts the message in the bottle and closes it.

He moves back to his office. He pushes the bottle in front of him. It is very difficult. His hands hurt, his knees hurt, and he has a lot of pain in his back.

It is lucky that Etienne did not close the doors to the balcony, he thinks.

Henri pulls himself along the floor and onto the balcony. He knows he only has one chance.

At the edge of the balcony, he pushes the bottle and watches it fall down to the sea.

If I am very lucky, the waves will carry the bottle to the beach near the little fishing village. Maybe someone will find it and come to rescue me.

Henri rests for a long time. Then he moves back to the kitchen and finds some water in a low cupboard. He pushes the water bottle along the floor to his bedroom. He cannot get into his bed, but he pulls the blankets down on top of him. Then he drinks a little. He is very weak. He is very tired. He falls asleep.

CHAPTER THREE

Isobel is walking along the beach. The sunset is beautiful today. She looks at the sea.

I'm so lucky to live here, she thinks. *But the tourists are all on the other beaches. No one comes here to this small fishing village. Nothing ever happens here. I want an adventure!*

She looks out at the sea. *I wonder about life on that island,* she thinks. Isobel wants to go to university and she wants to travel, but her family has no money.

She looks at the waves. Something in the water is shining.

What is that? she thinks.

She walks into the water and picks up a bottle.

There is piece of paper inside. It's a message in a bottle!

She takes the message out of the bottle and reads it.

---*Help me. I'm Henri Olivier on the island. Call Mr Berger's law office in Madrid. Telephone number 0123-454-676. And call the police. Emergency! SOS!*---

She looks out at the sea.

Henri Olivier. That is the rich man. He has the island over there.

From the coast, she can see the island a little.

This is very strange, she thinks.

Isobel runs home.

She shows the message to her friend Sergio.

"What should we do, Sergio?" she asks.

"I don't know. Maybe he is in danger. Or maybe it is a joke."

"Maybe we should go to the island," says Isobel. "Or call the police."

Sergio's cousin sees them.

"Hey, what are you two doing?" he asks.

Isobel doesn't like Sergio's cousin, Jose. He has many friends in the next town. He goes to bars a lot. He is always in trouble.

Jose takes the message from Sergio and reads it.

"My friend knows Henri Olivier's son," he says. "His name is Etienne."

Jose wants to be friends with Etienne. *This is my chance,* he thinks.

"I'm going to call my friend", he says.

He takes the bottle and message and goes away.

Isobel and Sergio look at each other.

I don't think this is a good idea," says Sergio.

"It's strange. Why didn't Henri Olivier write in the note 'call Etienne'?" asks Isobel. "Maybe Etienne is in trouble too. Maybe he needs help too."

"I don't know," says Sergio. "Etienne is a bad man. Many people are afraid of him. We should be careful. Maybe he has done something bad to his father."

They both look out to sea.

"Let's go to the island. Let's use your father's boat", says Isobel.

"When?" says Sergio.

"Tonight!" says Isobel. "Henri might be in danger! And I want an adventure!"

CHAPTER FOUR

Etienne is in Madrid.

He is in a bar. His phone rings. He listens carefully.

"What?" he says. "I'm coming back. Don't call the police. He is OK, but he has been strange recently. He is very old and there is a problem with his head. He gets crazy ideas."

He puts the phone down.

I don't believe that man sent a message in a bottle! He is a stupid man, he thinks. *I thought no one would go to the island and he would die. Now I must go back to island and kill him before anyone comes to help him.*

Etienne goes out of the bar and takes a taxi to the airport.

CHAPTER FIVE

Isobel and Sergio wait until it is dark. They go down to the harbour. They get into Sergio's father's boat.

It is very dark, but the water is calm. They can hear the sounds of the nightclubs and bars at the next beach.

The island is dark. They cannot see it.

"There must be trouble," says Isobel. "Usually, we can see lights on the island at night. But tonight, there are no lights."

They row into the water.

After 30 minutes, they are near the island and can see the high rocks and the dark shape of the house.

Isobel hears the sound of an engine.

"What's that?" she asks.

"It's a speedboat," says Sergio. They look at each other.

The speedboat comes closer.

"It's Etienne!" says Sergio. "He is the only person near here with a boat like that."

"Hey, what are you doing?" shouts Etienne.

"Er, nothing. We are just enjoying a romantic evening together," says Sergio.

Etienne looks at him. "Hey, I know you. You are Jose's cousin."

"Yeah," says Sergio.

"You found the note from my father."

"Yeah, we did. Is he OK?"

Etienne laughs.

"Don't worry, he's fine. But recently, he is strange. He says crazy things. I am here now, don't worry. Go back," says Etienne.

"Shall we call the police?" asks Isobel.

"No, no!" says Etienne.

Then he looks at Sergio.

"Your family has a fishing business. I know your father's business. It will have many problems if you call the police."

"What problems?" asks Isobel.

Etienne looks at her.

"Many problems!" he shouts. "Now go!"

Sergio and Isobel start rowing away. Etienne watches them. Then he turns his speedboat towards the island.

"I have a bad feeling," says Sergio.

"I have a bad feeling too," says Isobel. "The message did not say 'tell Etienne I am in trouble'."

"Something is wrong. I'm going to swim over to the island," says Sergio.

"Can I come with you?"

"No, you stay here on the boat. I will be back soon."

"Be careful," says Isobel.

Very quietly, Sergio jumps into the water and starts to swim to the island.

CHAPTER SIX

Isobel watches Sergio swim away through the dark sea.

Soon, she cannot see him at all. She waits for a long time. Thirty minutes pass. Then fifty minutes, then an hour. Isobel starts to worry.

What should I do? she thinks. *I am so worried about Sergio. Maybe something bad has happened. I will go and look for him.*

She rows towards the island. It is a very calm night, with no wind. After a while, she sees Etienne's speedboat. It is next to the steps that go up to the house. Isobel doesn't want to leave Sergio's father's boat near the speedboat. She rows around to another side of the island. It is a long way, but Isobel is a fisherman's daughter. She can row a boat very well. She finds a small beach. There are many trees. She gets out of the boat and pushes it through the water up onto the beach. Then she walks quietly through the trees. It is too dark. Isobel cannot see well. She is worried she will fall over. She cannot hear anything. The house is on the other side of the island, but the island is very small, so it is not so far away.

Where is Sergio? she thinks.

Then she stops. She can hear a noise.

What was that?

She stops and listens. The noise is in the trees. It is getting closer.

She feels very frightened. She turns around and starts to run back to the boat. The noise follows her. She runs faster. Something is chasing her. She sees the boat. Then, she falls. She sees the shadow of a man. He grabs her and puts his hand on her mouth.

She cannot scream.

"Isobel! What are you doing? I told you to stay in the boat!"

"I'm sorry! I was worried about you!" said Isobel.

"We will be in trouble!" says Sergio. Sergio takes Isobel's hand and they walk together back towards the trees. "We can hide here," says Sergio. "Sit down. We are both tired." They sit on the ground behind a tree.

"What happened? What did you see?" asks Isobel.

"It is very bad," says Sergio. "Henri is in danger."

"What danger?" asks Isobel. "How do you know?"

"I went up to the house. I found a door open. I heard Etienne shouting. I walked very quietly towards the noise. The old man and his son were in a bedroom. The old man was lying on the floor. Etienne is very angry, and he drank too much wine. He is like a crazy person. Henri asked his lawyer, Mr Berger, to give his money to an animal charity when he dies. But Mr Berger said Henri has to sign some papers. Etienne wants him to die before he can sign the papers. Etienne was hitting him. He said, 'I will kill you.'"

"So we must contact the police, and Mr Berger," says Isobel.

"I don't want to contact the police. Etienne will know that we told the police. He will destroy my father's business. We must contact Mr Berger. We must tell him to come here."

"But it will take him a long time to get here," says Isobel. "Henri Olivier will be dead before Mr Berger can come here."

"OK," says Sergio. "Henri Olivier's life is more important than my father's fishing business. But maybe there is another way. We will save Henri Olivier!"

"How are we going to do that?" asks Isobel.

"I don't know," says Sergio. "But we must go to the house."

CHAPTER SEVEN

Sergio and Isobel hurry towards the house.

"I have an idea," says Sergio. "You hide behind the house. I will go down to Etienne's speedboat. I will make a lot of noise. If we are lucky, Sergio will come down to the boat. When he is out of the house, you can run inside and help Henri Olivier."

"But Sergio," says Isobel. "You said Etienne was like a crazy person. It will be very dangerous. Maybe he will kill you!"

"I will be OK," says Sergio. "I think it is the only way to save Henri, but we have to hurry!"

The house is dark, but they can see a small light in one room.

"I think that is the old man's bedroom. When Etienne comes out of the house, you can go in," says Sergio.

"What are you going to do?" asks Isobel.

Sergio laughs. "Wait and see!"

Isobel hides at the back of the house. She watches Sergio walk towards the front of the house. It is so dark that very quickly Sergio disappears. She cannot see him anymore.

She is very frightened. But she waits. Suddenly there is a very loud noise. The sky becomes bright with an orange light.

She hears someone shouting inside the house. It is Etienne. He runs out of the house. "My boat! My boat!" He runs to the front of the house.

Isobel runs into the house. She runs to the room with the light. Henri Olivier is lying on the floor. His face is bleeding. He looks very bad.

"Mr Olivier!" says Isobel. "My name is Isobel. I have come to help you. Can you stand up?"

"No," says Henri. "My back is very bad and I am ill." Isobel helps him to drink some water.

She is worried. "We must hide," she says. "Etienne will come back very soon."

"I'm sorry," says the old man. "Don't worry about me. Please run away and hide."

"I can't do that," says Isobel.

She can hear shouting. The shouting is coming closer to the house. She can hear Etienne's voice, but she can't hear Sergio's voice.

Sergio! I hope Sergio is OK. What can I do? She looks around the room. She sees a lamp and picks it up. She stands next to the door and waits.

"You stupid man! I am going to kill you!"

When Etienne runs into the room, Isobel hits him very hard with the lamp. He falls down and Isobel jumps on his back.

"Isobel! Isobel!" says Sergio. "I tried to catch him down at the boat, but he was too quick and strong!"

"Help me," shouts Isobel. "I can't hold him!"

Sergio holds Etienne down on the floor. "Go and find some rope," he shouts. Isobel finds some rope in the kitchen. She helps Sergio tie Etienne's arms and legs. Then Sergio pulls him out of the bedroom and into another room.

Sergio comes back and says, "I will go for help. Can you stay with Mr Olivier? You will be safe now."

Isobel is not happy, but she says, "OK." She looks at Sergio. He is very wet and very dirty. His hands and face are black. "What did you do?" asks Isobel.

"I will tell you later. But now I must go. I will take Etienne's speedboat. It will be much quicker."

Isobel sits on the floor next to Mr Olivier and holds his hand. The old man smiles at her. "Thank you. You are a very brave young woman." He closes his eyes and doesn't talk anymore.

About forty minutes later, many people come to the island. There are doctors and policemen. Sergio comes with the policemen. The doctors take Mr Olivier away to a hospital in a big town. The policemen take Etienne to prison.

CHAPTER EIGHT

The next day, Isobel asks Sergio how he made the loud noise and bright orange light.

"It was a very good idea," she says. "Etienne heard the noise and saw the light. He ran out of the house very quickly. What did you do?"

Sergio laughs. "I swam out to the speedboat. I found oil. I found a lighter. I found paper and an empty wine bottle. I made a firebomb. I threw it very far from the boat and it exploded. It was a very good bomb!"

A week later, Mr Berger comes to the little fishing village. He wants to talk to Sergio and Isobel.

"Mr Olivier is still in hospital," he says. "He is very ill. The doctors say maybe he will be able to walk again, but he must stay in hospital for a long time."

"I am sorry," says Isobel. "I thought he was a very nice man."

"He is a very nice man," says Mr Berger. "But he is very sad about his son. When his son was a young boy, Mr Olivier was working very hard to make money. He was always away from home. So he feels bad. He thinks he was a bad father."

"I do not agree. I think Mr Olivier tried hard to be a good father, but his son is a bad person," says Isobel.

Mr Berger smiles. "But I came to talk to you about other things. Mr Olivier told me to give all his money to an animal charity when he dies. Now he has another idea. When he dies, he wants me to give his money to this village. He wants to build a new school and maybe a small hospital."

"That would be a very good thing for this village," says Sergio.

"But Mr Olivier wants to give you some money while he is still alive. He wants to give you enough money to go to university. Would you like that?"

"Yes," says Isobel.

"No," says Sergio.

Mr Berger laughs. "OK. I will tell Mr Olivier than you would like to go to university, Isobel. But Sergio, what do you want?"

"I want to stay here. I want to go fishing. This is my life and I like it," says Sergio.

"OK. How about a new fishing boat?" says Mr Berger.

"A new fishing boat! For my family! That's wonderful!" Sergio is very happy.

Isobel is happy too. "Before I found the bottle on the beach, I was unhappy. I wanted to go to university. I wanted an adventure. I got the adventure, and now I can go to university."

"And my family will be very happy to have a new fishing boat," says Sergio. "The message in the bottle was very good for us."

"It was very good for Mr Olivier too," says Mr Berger. "The message in the bottle saved his life."

THANK YOU

Thank you for reading Message in a Bottle. (Word count: 3,872) We hope you enjoyed it.

There are quizzes about this book on our free study site I Talk You Talk Press EXTRA. http://italk-youtalk.com

If you would like to read more graded readers, please visit our website http://www.italkyoutalk.com

Other Level 2 graded readers include
Adventure in Rome
Andre's Dream
A Passion for Music
Christmas Tales
Danger in Seattle
Don't Come Back
Finders Keepers…
John Sees a Murder
Marcy's Bakery
Men's Konkatsu Tales
Murder on Whale Island
Salaryman Secrets!
Stories for Halloween
The Perfect Wedding
The House in the Forest

The School on Bolt Street
Train Travel
Trouble in Paris
Women's Konkatsu Tales
Who's There?

ABOUT THE AUTHOR

I Talk You Talk Press is an award-winning Japan-based publisher of language textbooks, graded readers and language learning/teaching resources.

Our team is made up of highly experienced language teachers and translators, who have all studied at least one additional language to an advanced level.

This experience enables us to design our materials from the perspective of both the teacher and the learner. We consult with both teachers and language learners when designing our textbooks and graded readers, and test our materials extensively in the classroom before publication.

We are a fast-growing press, and currently publish graded readers for learners of English. We publish new graded readers monthly.